The Life of Little Nakita

Nikki Blaq

Mission: To Proclaim Transformation and Truth
Publisher: Transformed Publishing, Cocoa, FL
Website: www.transformedpublishing.com
Email: transformedpublishing@gmail.com

ISBN: 978-1-953241-52-8 (paperback)
ISBN: 978-1-953241-53-5 (Ebook)

DEDICATION

I dedicate this book to everyone who has believed in me and encouraged me to face my fears and be transparent about my growth.

I couldn't have completed this goal without my husband and my kids, who motivated me through all my flaws and failures; my niece, who put in the time and effort to edit my work; my family and friends; and last but not least, my mother, who is my #1 supporter.

I dedicate this book to every person
who has ever felt like giving up on themselves.

To everyone who has ever given up
on their goals and dreams.

To everyone who thought that they
couldn't succeed past their mistakes.

To everyone who has ever thought that they
were worthless and would never amount to anything.

-Nakita

Words of Encouragement

- ✓ Know who you are
- ✓ Be true to who you are
- ✓ Know your worth
- ✓ Always believe in yourself
- ✓ Never let other people tell you who you are
- ✓ Know that you have a purpose in this world

Quotes I Live
By *Nikki Blaq*

My Golden Rules:

Never let anyone make choices for you
that will damage your destiny.

Remember that if you don't manage
your time properly, you'll lose opportunities
(i.e. growth, greatness, change, etc.).

There are 2 roads to travel to reach your destiny,
pick one!
(Failure or Success) (Give up or Succeed)

TABLE OF CONTENTS

Preface

Hi there,

I'd like to properly introduce myself. My name is Nakita! I'm a proud mother of three children, a set of beautiful identical twin girls and a handsome young son, and also an awesome wife to a wonderful husband. I was born and raised in the small town of Cocoa, Florida, not to be confused with Cocoa Beach, as many often do. I've always been a small-town girl with big dreams because I'm an avid believer that *there's always room for improvement.*

In my adulthood, I took a leap of faith and moved to the city of Orlando, Florida. As a result of taking that risk, my work ethic has allowed me to achieve proficiency in several trades and even gained me the opportunity to work in executive positions within Corporate America. As of now, I'm a Licensed Private Investigator with over a decade of professional experience. I'm also actively working in the Criminal Justice field as a Licensed Bail Bondsman (woman) and in the medical field as a Medical Assistant.

Enough of my present life, let's rewind to the years when I had big dreams and a lot of fears. As kids, we have fantasies about what we want our lives to become once we're all grown up. From my experience, I can tell you the plans we set for our lives aren't always God's plans. In my opinion, it's best to trust the process and remain in the race with a positive attitude. My grandmother always told me, "What doesn't kill you will only make you stronger."

Where I'm from I was taught, what goes on in your house stays in your house. But when you have overcome tragedies, abuse, or trauma, it's good to talk about it. Your testimony may help save another person from pain, suffering, or heartache, not to mention revive someone who is dealing with self-esteem issues. The goal of telling my story is to give someone else hope.

I decided to speak my truth openly and freely so if you don't mind, I'll like to share my story with you and hope it enlightens your mood and helps you mentally, spiritually, emotionally, and physically.

1
THE LIFE OF LITTLE NAKITA

When I was a little girl
I dreamed of traveling the world
Joining the Airforce
Taking control over - my choice
Of where my life will go

I wanted to be rich
I was tired of being poe
Not to mention growing up in the ghetto
Mom on drugs so I had no room to grow

She loved me but couldn't provide
I loved her but I was tired
Of living the way, we lived
I packed my things and hit the hills
To which cometh my help
Straight to Granny's house is where I felt
Warmth, love, and attention
But she didn't play so I had to listen
I'll take that over everything

Next chapter I couldn't sustain
And the goals and dreams that I had
Went down the drain, I became bad
Selling drugs and chasing money
Smoking weed thinking everything was funny
I became a momma to my sister
I was happy until along came mister

Wanting to be the man
Crazy as a pitbull, mean as a rattlesnake
I wasn't scared of that man NAH wait
He was my uncle, but we loved him as a dad
He was so controlling that really made me mad
He took my sister out of my home
I wanted to hurt him, but I left it alone

The babies were born
I wasn't ready to be a mother
I had become a woman scorned
I was mean to my children, and everybody else
I was a single mom with little to no help
Because I picked an A-hole to be their dad
He couldn't stay free which was so sad

I remembered my dreams
My brother-n-law and family became my team
I had support, love, and motivation
The twins were the reason I went back to finish my education
I received my diploma at 25
Finished college with a baby on the inside
Long story short keep your goals and dreams
Times get hard but it's not as it seems
I grew and I grew
I appreciate life and I walked in my truth

I am an ex convicted felon
With a gun and a career because I didn't mind failing
There're many more mountains to climb, but for now
I'm claiming everything that's mine
My business, my husband, my children, my success,
My wealth, and my life because I am truly blessed

My nieces and nephews will overcome like me,
Because I go to GOD about them faithfully
Life is a game with limited mistakes
Make right decisions don't throw your life away
You may not care about it today
But everything that you do paves the way
For your destiny and your future
Be careful with your choices
Them consequences can be crucial

By *Nikki Blaq*

Journaling Prompt:

- ❖ *Have you been going through life carrying hate in your heart and negative thoughts in your mind?*

- ❖ *How do you handle your thoughts, failures, pain, and / or issues?*

Let them go!

Please release that toxic energy from within you. One method to release energy is to talk about it and if there's no one who you can trust with your personal information then write it down.

Writing poems has become my form of therapy. Whenever I write down the things that have been bothering me, I always feel ten times better afterwards. I always release any thoughts that are negatively controlling my mind.

Get rid of all bitterness, rage, anger, harsh words, and slander, as well as all types of evil behavior.
-Ephesians 4:31

Hatred stirs up quarrels, but love makes up for all offenses.
-Proverbs 10:12

Don't just pretend to love others. Really love them. Hate what is wrong. Hold tightly to what is good.
-Romans 12:9

Love in Action!

Date: ___________________

Date: _________________________

Date: _______________________

1990's were the best years,
They brought me pain, laughter, and tears
During these times I was taught many lessons
I experienced a lot, but I held my confessions

I started middle school, boy was I crushing
It was full of fine boys every day I was blushing
Couldn't wait to walk through them gates
Or get to the gym to sit back and just gape
At the boys playing basketball
I was a big flirt, if I got their number I didn't call

We had pagers back then,
To get in touch with your friends
43770 said *hello* - 90 said *go*
41 was *hi*, those were the good ole days
That's when .10 cents bought you a pie
2 dollars would get you a bag full of snacks
By the end of 7th period,
I was full and made all my money back

1995 was all the way live, I had become that big 1-5
I jumped off the porch chasing a check
That's just the beginning I'm not finished yet

1996 you couldn't tell me I wasn't it,
I was locked in with an all boy click
And my Ace boon coon
The 2 sportiest young females when we walked in a room
TPG became my street family

When I got shot, I became a straight no limit soldier
I didn't know it wasn't cool until I got older
I used to brag check my war wound
But I was thankful my grandma lived in her prayer room

This is the year 2Pac got killed
I was balling in Orlando, the whole city was ill
My sissy gave me Chrissy
That was my 1st car
You couldn't tell me nothing pulling up at Cocoa High

She dropped 2 nuggets in my mouth
I became a real street chick
Representing the dirty south
Grill shining pockets straight

So, I'll jump over to **1998**
I copped a Buick white insides and loud pipes
That's when I really became the omnipotent Nikki Blaq
I was also called Ballette and Black
Cause I was in the streets,
Hustling smoking weed and selling crack

That year I became grown,
And moved out of my grandma's home
Lost my virginity, man that was wrong
I lived in hotel after hotel the dude I was with stayed in jail
8 months later I was pregnant and alone
The smart thing to do was go back home
My grandma welcomed me with open arms
To her I could cause no harm

We got our 1st apartment living the family life
This cheater's side chick stabbed him with a knife
Life was no longer what it seemed

I felt like I was living in a horrible dream
Carrying 2 babies on the inside of me
Wanting to change my life and be totally free

From the streets, because the streets don't love me
Not even the people who are in 'em
This is a game that everybody wants to be winning

1999 things seemed fine
I had my babies and got back on the grind
It wasn't until I put the police on a high-speed chase
That I realized my life was heading the wrong way
My twins were 6 months old
I could have gotten killed that night running from TROLL
When I got out of the county jail
I promised myself the streets can go straight to hell
I have 2 little people who need me
And I'm going to be the best mother that I can be

I got a job,
It wasn't permanent it was too hard
Listening to someone telling me what to do
I packed up my things and said forget you
Back to the block, all I knew was selling rocks
I can smoke, make money, and have it my way

Dude, back in jail this isn't going to work
I'm back on somebody's job man this really hurts
I made up in my mind, I'm done this time
These kids need me
At least one of their parents must be free
I stuck with it and chose my babies

By *Nikki Blaq*

Journaling Prompt:

- ❖ *Can you recall your best years growing up? Write them down. Enjoy reminiscing in those moments.*

- ❖ *Which years are most memorable to you?*

The 1990's were the best years of my life. I was starting to grow up. As a result of growing up, I was beginning to figure out what I liked, what I didn't like, what my interests were, what my goals were, and what motivated me.

The things I learned became important life lessons for me. I was being taught to understand that my choices came with consequences.

Life has changed so much since my teenage years. Think about what electronics you had in your younger years and compare it to now, i.e., various technology, the economy, money, gaming systems, etc.

> This is the day the Lord has made. We will rejoice and be glad in it.
>
> -Psalm 118:24

> When I was a child, I spoke and thought and reasoned as a child. But when I grew up, I put away childish things.
>
> -1 Corinthians 13:11

Date: _______________________

Date: _______________________

Date: ______________________

3
A MOTHER'S HAT

My entire life I wanted a big family
With 10 kids like Eddie Murphy

I passed over all the good guys
So, I only have 3 which are my golden prize
I wouldn't trade them for anything
I'm a proud mother with no shame
Not even of their lifestyle
I stand up quick to support my child

They will never guess my position
I stand firm with them, and I listen
Sometimes I am their friend
But mostly to the twins

My baby boy is somewhat special
He was conceived in a 5-minute wrestle (lol)
My kids changed my life
I could be dead, or in jail because I wasn't living right

Because of their truth I had to regroup
I was given a second chance
To be a better mother as I enhanced

My love and affection
To build stronger connections
With the girls
Truth be told my kids are my world
I don't know where I would be
If it wasn't for my triple T's
Being a mother is the greatest gift
I pray when I get old, they do not shift

And throw me into a nursing home
From all the things they felt I did wrong
I dedicated my best years to my kids
I don't regret it, I'll do it again

Now it's time for mommy to live
I now have a husband I can relax and chill
I'm still too young to be a Nanna
I'm not keeping no babies or changing no pampers

Your stepdad and I have plans
To travel the world and roam some lands
But I'll be your best support
Catch you at any time, if you come up short

I'm not the perfect mother
But I tried my best
I did what I had to do
Their character speaks for the rest
By *Nikki Blaq*

Journaling Prompt:

- ❖ *Do you have kids? Describe your thoughts toward them.*

Make sure you show your children that they're loved and supported. It makes a huge difference in their lives, their self-esteem, and their intellectuality.

I must admit parenting is hard. It surely doesn't come with instructions or a brochure. My parenting came from day-to-day trials and errors. I raised my children based upon my traditional upbringing. However, as my daughters grew older, they expressed to me how I made them feel belittled growing up, without a voice or an opinion.

My advice is, *what may have worked generations ago to raise a child has to be updated and modernized.* The new generation isn't as tough as we were growing up. They're a little fragile, some privileged, and others lack respect. Times have changed and some of the tough love and harshness can damage a child.

Use the parenting style that best fits your household, or that fits your child's personality. Some kids get in order by a look, others a stern tone, but there is always one who those methods don't apply to.

> Those who spare the rod of discipline hate their children. Those who love their children care enough to discipline them.
>
> -Proverbs 13:24

> Direct your children onto the right path, and when they are older, they will not leave it.
>
> -Proverbs 22:6

Date: ______________________

Date: _______________________

Date: ___________________

4
LETTER TO MY UNBORN

I regret every day - for making the mistake
Of not giving you a chance at life - and letting you be great

At times I sit, and cry and I ask myself, "Why?"

You would have been 15, living the American dream
Being the best cheerleader or on the football team

I heard your heartbeat, and I will never forget
I wanted you so badly, you were conceived after a bad split

My ex was mad about you - he beat me until I was black & blue
I didn't know if you would have medical conditions
So, I terminated my pregnancy thinking that was the best decision

I lost you on my 27th birthday
I swear that pain will never go away

I will always love you my unborn child
If I could rewind the time, you'll be here now

I repent and I hope you forgive me for this sin
I love you so much, until we meet again

By *Nikki Blaq*

Journaling Prompt:

- ❖ *Have you aborted a child for one reason or another?*

- ❖ *Have you forgiven yourself and asked God for forgiveness?*

- ❖ *Have you made a regretful decision you wish you could change?*

When you're unsure about a situation, pray about it before you act. Do what's in your gut because that's usually the right decision.

This was the hardest decision of my life. And I still regret it, but I have forgiven myself and I've repented for my sin.

Take a second and free yourself by asking for forgiveness.

["]He will wipe every tear from their eyes, and there will be no more death or sorrow or crying or pain. All these things are gone forever."

-Revelation 21:4

The Lord is close to the brokenhearted; he rescues those whose spirits are crushed.

-Psalm 34:18

So you have sorrow now, but I will see you again; then you will rejoice, and no one can rob you of that joy.

-John 16:22

God blesses those who mourn, or they will be comforted.

-Matthew 5:4

Date: _____________________

Date: _______________________

Date: ___________________

5
MY STRUGGLES

Throughout my years, I shed so many tears

Some for the bad some for the good
But regardless of the reason I never really understood
Why I had to struggle so hard
I didn't like the hand I was dealt, but I always played the right card

Which kept me in the game, I'll lose, I'll win but the facts still remain
I wasn't in control of my life, but I felt everything I did was right

Until one day I decided to seek GOD

And everything started making sense
I have a divine purpose,
God was rewarding me for my accomplishments

Through my hard times I try not to complain
I thank God for coming out of the rain

One day I will reach the shelter
Where there is peace and love
Life will be so much better

I'm a work in progress so
I thank the Lord, for helping me do my best

By *Nikki Blaq*

Journaling Prompt:

- ❖ *What are your struggles?*

- ❖ *How do you deal with them?*

- ❖ *How have your struggles made you stronger?*

- ❖ *In what ways have you developed strength from life's troublesome events?*

No one wants to struggle and live a hard life. It doesn't seem fair when you're looking at others eating around you and enjoying life. However, everything isn't always what it looks like. Run your own race and take your time getting to the finish line so you can enjoy each blessing in its time.

Enjoy your life!

["]This is my command—be strong and courageous! Do not be afraid or discouraged. For the Lord your God is with you wherever you go."

-Joshua 1:9

Yet what we suffer now is nothing compared to the glory he will reveal to us later.

-Romans 8:18

Date: ______________________

Date: _______________________

Date: _______________________

6
ABUSE

Don't be confused about ABUSE
if it doesn't feel right save the excuse

Recognize the actions and the effect
If you're not uncomfortable it's not that bad yet

When there's ongoing patterns and the multiple apologies
It's at the stage they're using reverse sociology
They will hit you and say I'm sorry

Make themselves cry as they're telling you this lie

A narcissistic demonic soul is what they are
Controlling, manipulative and will blame you for your scars

Degrade your character as if you did something wrong
While battling with their guilt all along

I experienced several types of ABUSE
From family, friends' partners with loose screws

My ABUSE started out verbally
Before you knew it the man, I was dating started hurting me

The worse ABUSE is torture and mental
It starts without your knowing silent and gentle

Before you know it, you're scared for your life
There're many nights I slept with a knife

Beneath my pillow, ready for whatever was to come
But I wasn't expecting for him to have a gun

People judge you on the outside
Not knowing what's happening on the inside

If you ask me, it's best
To keep your enemy close so that you can rest
I rather have him here to know what he's thinking
Instead of walking out the door and someone find me stinking

By *Nikki Blaq*

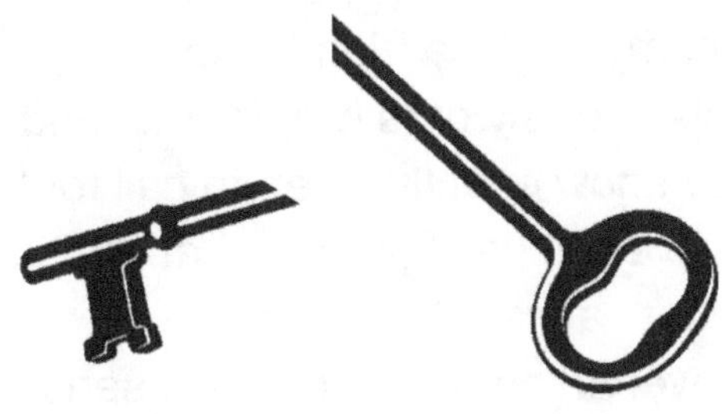

Journaling Prompt:

- ❖ *Describe an abusive relationship you have been in.*

- ❖ *Are you in an abusive relationship? Explain.*

- ❖ *What are signs of abuse?*

Abuse isn't always physical. Abuse can be verbal.

In my opinion, or shall I say from my own personal experience, mental abuse has been the worst for me by far. Physical wounds and scars heal, but verbal abuse plays over and over in the mind. It messes with your self-esteem, your confidence, and most importantly it depletes self-love.

Things you should know and do when you're in an abusive relationship:

- ✓ Tell somebody! Don't be ashamed because it's not your fault!
- ✓ Always have a safety plan. Keep a bag packed with essentials (toothbrush, toothpaste, 2-3 days' worth of clothes for you and your children, needed hygiene products, cash, and a phone charger) just in case you must camp out at a friend's house.
- ✓ Establish code words with friends and family members so they know exactly when to call for help.
- ✓ Learn your abuser (know what makes him / her mad and what calms them down).
- ✓ Take everything he or she says seriously!

Date: ___________________

Date: _______________________

Date: ___________________

7
HEALING

I used to be broken, toxic, and angry
I wished a man would think that he could tame me

I would use them, mislead them
Have fun then leave them

Get attached fall in love
Heck nah, I didn't need them

Hurt people hurt people
It's not fair but it's lethal

A hurt man played with my heart
He tortured it and ripped it apart

Made it hard for another man
My heart became fragile like quicksand

My mission became to please them
And tease them
Then break their heart for no reason

That game got old, and the nights got cold
I was really losing
Single and left with their souls

I was never committed but they couldn't let go
Now that I'm older who's really keeping the score
I didn't win in the end
But you couldn't tell me that back then
Another had my soul, so I was trying to fill it in

With the ones who love me, hoping I'll be free
Move on with my life, love someone truly

And become their wife
It took many years to become free
I prayed for God to release me

I wanted to reclaim my heart
And make it pure
I recited that prayer for one straight year

Prepare my husband for me, God I will wait patiently

Prepare me for my husband
I promise to love him with less fussing and cussing

There're days I want to cuss him out
And there're days I want to scream and shout

But I promised God, 'I will honor my marriage with love'
If the man who He sends me was a God-fearing reformed thug

Some may get it others will not
But the characteristics of that man will give you everything he got

He gives **love, protection**, and **provides** 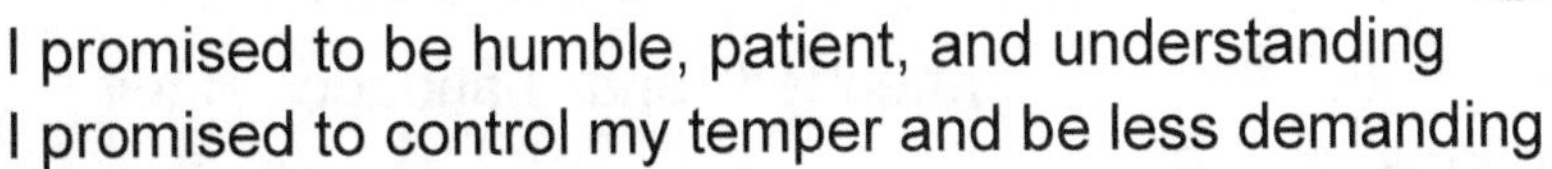
If anything jumps off that man is going to ride

I promised to be humble, patient, and understanding
I promised to control my temper and be less demanding

This new life is a challenge
But I'm willing to give it my all to keep it balanced

I've let my guard down and opened my heart
How it turns out is the way he plays his part

SoulSnatcher
By *Nikki Blaq*

Journaling Prompt:

- ❖ *Describe something you went through that you thought you'd never heal from.*

- ❖ *How is your journey of healing from a traumatic experience affecting your current relationships?*

Pray about it and ask God to help you heal. Time heals all things, some faster than others. Healing is a process; it doesn't happen overnight.

It took thirteen plus years for my heart to be healed. My heart was broken. I was poisoned by bitterness; I became mean and angry. I couldn't trust any man.

But I wanted to love and be loved. So, I started fixing myself on the inside by getting to know myself and learning what I really wanted in life. I started applying positive energy by intentionally giving what I wanted in return, to everyone I came in contact with.

I gave respect - time - attention - understanding

and I received it all back in greater measure.

He heals the brokenhearted and bandages their wounds.

-Psalm 147:3

"I am leaving you with a gift—peace of mind and heart. And the peace I give is a gift the world cannot give. So don't be troubled or afraid.["]

-John 14:27

Have compassion on me, Lord, for I am weak. Heal me, Lord, for my bones are in agony.

-Psalm 6:2

Date: _______________________

Date: ________________________

Date: _______________________

8
MY SOUL IS SEARCHING

I was raised as a Baptist, but my spirit felt captured

So, I set out to be free, in an environment that I could be me
As one of God's creations, I was open to praise with any nation

Then it was come as you are, bow to Jesus and give Him your heart
I was feeling that, until one day I felt a tap

I looked around and seen no one
Whoever this was, thought it was fun

To whisper in my ear, I did not see them, but I could hear
The voices amongst the drums
That made my spirit feel warm

It was my ancestors getting my attention, I love the feeling might I mention
I felt alive and pure, but I heard another voice in my ear

You're not supposed to entertain the dead
But they were messing with me, putting things in my head

I was enjoying that life, but I knew it wasn't right

I walked away with my head hung low
I looked back at them and said I got to go

On the inside I was bawling, but the Lord said you have a calling
One that I have ordained follow Me, you'll never be the same
God has a plan for me to walk on new land
I accepted my purpose, I no longer feel worthless

I will conquer this, and be the next powerful Evangelist

By *Nikki Blaq*

Journaling Prompt:

- ❖ *Where does your soul rest?*

- ❖ *Are you satisfied?*

Most children grow up serving the God who was taught to them. However, when they get older, they have the choice to find out what makes their soul feel free and fed.

My soul wasn't getting what it needed and that sparked my journey to search for a religion that made me happy and feel good.

I was unfulfilled until I realized the connection had to be received within me. Looking back, I now know the misconception: I wasn't focusing on a relationship with GOD, I was focusing on pleasing my flesh.

. . . And this is the secret: Christ lives in you . . .

-Colossians 1:27

And we know that God causes everything to work together for the good of those who love God and are called according to his purpose for them.

-Romans 8:28

If we live, it's to honor the Lord. And if we die, it's to honor the Lord. So whether we live or die, we belong to the Lord.

-Romans 14:8

Date: ___________________

Date: ________________________

Date: _______________________

9
LORD, CAN YOU HEAR ME?

We go through things in life, that don't seem right
You pray, you fast, and you still must fight

Life is an endless struggle
God, why me? They hurt me and I still love them

I started giving and I'm willing

Looking for nothing in return, only Your Grace and Mercy

I've learned to do what is pleasing to GOD
Lord knows this thing called life is very hard

I look to the hills which cometh my help
I've sat so long I think my help has left

Am I not passing the test You give?
I know I need correction on how I should live

I cannot do this on my own
I still need guidance even though I'm grown

Comfort Your child I'm breaking down
Sitting still waiting to hear the sound

The sound of Your voice
Reminding me of my greatest choice

Help me O God I've changed for the better
Send me a sign or even a letter

Letting me know that You are still here
I'm walking in faith and running from fear

HELLO GOD, ARE YOU NEAR?   By *Nikki Blaq*

Journaling Prompt:

❖ *Does life seem to weigh you down and cause you to wonder if God hears your prayers or your cries? Explain.*

God hears your silent cries:

He's just preparing you for your blessing.

Don't look at your life situation as what it is now, because God is working on what you cannot see.

Yes, that statement is easier said than done, right? Trust me, I know. I've been in that particular situation more than once or twice. But there have always been better days to follow.

And if you do not carry your own cross and follow me, you cannot be my disciple.

-Luke 14:27

Don't be afraid, for I am with you.
Don't be discouraged, for I am your God.
I will strengthen you and help you.
I will hold you up with my victorious right hand.

-Isaiah 41:10

Date: ___________________

Date: _______________________

Date: _______________________

10
YOU CAN DO IT

I had so much hurt in my heart,
Because your habits tore us apart

You chose your life over mine,
And left me and my sisters all behind

But you have made a huge turnaround
You still fall short, but you never let us down

I love you now more than ever
You can do it, so never say never

I'm here when you need me, just a phone call away
If I don't answer just get on your knees and pray

God will answer your call that's who saved your life after all

By *Nikki Blaq*

Covid had a deadly effect on so many people's lives in 2020. By the grace of God, He used that time of despair to save my mother's life. My mom finally kicked her drug addiction. It was the happiest day of my life. I prayed for that moment to come for over twenty years.

She has become my best friend. There were days I thought this moment would never happen. I'm a living witness that prayer changes things. I never gave up.

Journaling Prompt:

❖ *Do you have a family member who has had or currently has a drug addiction? Describe the effects it has had on you.*

Do not give up on your loved ones!

I'm here to tell you, "Do not give up on your loved ones!" Some people take longer than others to change. Even if they *may* never change, continue to love them, and remind them that they are somebody.

Today, step out of your comfort zone and take that family member out to eat or spend time with them. You never know what type of effect it will have on their life. Positive energy changes the mood of others.

Date: _______________________

Date: _______________________

Date: ___________________

11
MY MOMMA CLEAN NOW

I got my momma back; 2020 she got off crack

We have a relationship we never had,
I'm so proud of her, I'm so glad

She chose to live and kick her habit,
I pray every night she remains a savage

She went cold turkey in a day's time,
She was diagnosed with COPD and thought she was dying

I thank GOD for delivering her
We were given a second chance that's for sure

By *Nikki Blaq*

Journaling Prompt:

❖ *What is the biggest miracle that has taken place in your life? Record your thanksgiving.*

For I can do everything through Christ, who gives me strength.

-Philippians 4:13

Even when I walk through the darkest valley, I will not be afraid, for you are close beside me. Your rod and your staff protect and comfort me.

-Psalm 23:4

The Lord is my light and my salvation—so why should I be afraid? The Lord is my fortress, protecting me from danger, so why should I tremble?

-Psalm 27:1

For God has not given us a spirit of fear and timidity, but of power, love, and self-discipline.

-2 Timothy 1:7

Date: ________________________

Date: _______________________

Date: _______________________

Reflections

My hope is the techniques I have provided, which helped me learn how to love myself and express who I am without being bothered by other people's opinions, motive you to find your inner strength.

Hopefully, after reading my truth and self-healing process, you have gained healing and growth.

I would like to thank you for reading my book. I hope some, if not the majority, of my poems have given you different insight into your life's struggles and encouraged you to love everything about yourself - inside and out. Remember, you can do all things in life as long as you believe *it* will happen.

Think about these questions, as you continue to reflect:

- ❖ *Think about the dreams you had growing up. Which dreams have you achieved?*

- ❖ *Which dreams have you not yet achieved? What are some ways you can accomplish these dreams?*

Maybe your life turned out better than you imagined when you were a kid. Now ask yourself:

- ❖ *Are you thankful for the good in your life? Explain.*

- ❖ *Do you complain about what you don't have? Do you take wealth, happiness, or success for granted? Are you boastful or helpful? Explain.*

- ❖ *Stop and write God a 'Thank You'.*

Date: ___________________

Date: _______________________

Date: ___________________

I used to think struggling was failure, but I learned to realize, *failure is preparation!* It prepared me to survive. And it prepared me to be grateful for everything I have. Struggling also built my character, strengthened my mind, enlightened my heart to care for others, and taught me structure, organization, and most of all patience.

Take these 5 words -

pray. faith. give. patience. & forgiveness

apply them to your everyday living.
I promise you; your life will change for the better.

- ❖ *PRAY - daily, tell God what you need in your life.*

- ❖ *FAITH - believe you will have all that you asked for*

- ❖ *GIVE - God time out of your day. Give Him a simple 'thank you', an 'I love You', or simply talk to Him as you would a friend or family member.*

- ❖ *PATIENCE - take your time, do not rush. Everything happens at the right time and during the right season for the right reason.*

- ❖ *FORGIVENESS - We do wrong daily, but if you forgive and ask for forgiveness and mean it, you'll make better decisions in life because your mind will become free and open to change. Holding grudges and being angry only clouds your mind. A cloudy mind will lead you to make horrible decisions.*

Give thanks to the Lord, for he is good! His faithful love endures forever.

-1 Chronicles 16:34

Since we are receiving a Kingdom that is unshakable, let us be thankful and please God by worshiping him with holy fear and awe.

-Hebrews 12:28

Let all that I am praise the Lord; with my whole heart, I will praise his holy name. Let all that I am praise the Lord; may I never forget the good things he does for me. He forgives all my sins and heals all my diseases. He redeems me from death and crowns me with love and tender mercies.

-Psalm 103:1-4

Do everything without complaining and arguing, so that no one can criticize you. Live clean, innocent lives as children of God, shining like bright lights in a world full of crooked and perverse people.

-Philippians 2:14-15

Date: _______________________

Date: ______________________

Date: ___________________

About the Author

Throughout my life, I have climbed many mountains, and I have failed many times. However, not once did I ever give up. I've heard the word 'no' more times than I could ever count. 'No' never stopped me from continuing my test to earn that 'yes'. The thousands and thousands of tests I've taken have become my testimony. I've never given anyone the power to determine the choices that I have the right to make. I take full accountability for my actions, mistakes, and failures.

Don't get me wrong, I've made plenty of mistakes in my life. From those mistakes, I've learned that excuses only hold you back from your purpose and stop your growth. I vowed to enjoy every moment of my life, even when things aren't going as planned, because I am a true witness to the fact that there's a lesson in every situation, circumstance, and silent moment in your life. During those silent times when I couldn't see any breakthrough happening or light to shine on my darkest days, I always made a greater version of myself.

Stay Connected

Please contact Nakita, via email, for speaking engagements, book signings, bulk book orders, or to share your testimony:

Nikkiblaq.author@gmail.com

 **Connect on Instagram:**
@Msblaqroyalsigning

@msblaqroyalservices

New Release, Coming Winter 2024:
Life has Gotten Better